Miss Bea's Rainy Day

Louisa Harding

ROWAN

It's a rainy day today,
too wet to play outside.

Rainy day sweater instructions page 28

Oscar doesn't mind,
he likes to sit and read his books.

'What else can we do?'
Hannah builds a tower, but it tumbles to the floor.

Joseph gets out the train set,
but the track does not go far.

'Cheer up everybody',
Hannah draws a smiling face.

Smiling Jacket instructions page 36

'Let's race the cars across the room',
but they go too fast to catch.

Racing sweater instructions page 38

Miss Bea bakes heart shaped cookies
but she gets the flour everywhere.

Cookie Sweater instructions page 40

Hannah pours the tea for two
but no-one comes to play.

Tea for Two Sweater instructions page 42

'I think the rain is going to stop,
but I must wash up the dishes'.

Thinking dress instructions page 44

'Come on everybody, let's go out to play'
but take your umbrella, it just might rain again.

Out to Play coat instructions page 46

The Knitting Patterns
Infomation Page

Introduction

The knitwear in 'Miss Bea's Rainy Day' has been designed using cables which add interest and texture to your knitting. With beginner knitters in mind we have included a techniques section about cabling on page 27.
The garment shapes are simple to knit and are knitted in one colour.

The knitting patterns

Each pattern has a chart and simple written instructions that have been colour coded making the different sizes easier to identify. E.g. if you are knitting age 2–3 years follow the instructions in red where you are given a choice. The patterns are laid out as follows:

Age/Size Diagrams

The ages given and the corresponding diagrams are a guide only. The measurements for each knitted piece are shown in a size diagram at the start of every pattern. As all children vary make sure you choose the right garment size, do this by measuring an item of your child's clothing you like the fit of. Choose the instruction size accordingly. If still unsure, knit a larger size, as children always grow.

Yarn

This indicates the amount of yarn needed to complete the design.

Needles

Listed are the suggested knitting needles used to make the garment. The smaller needles are usually used for edgings or ribs, the larger needles for the main body fabric.

Buttons/Zips

This indicates the number of buttons or length of zip needed to fasten the finished garment.

Tension

Tension is the single most important factor when you begin knitting. The fabric tension is written for example as 20 sts x 28 rows to 10cm measured over stocking stitch using 4 mm (US 6) needles. Each pattern is worked out mathematically, if the correct tension is not achieved the garment pieces will not measure the size stated in the diagram.

Before embarking on knitting your garment we recommend you check your tension as follows: Using the needle size given cast on 5 –10 more stitches than stated in the tension, and work 5 –10 more rows. When you have knitted your tension square lay it on a flat surface, place a rule or tape measure horizontally, count the number of stitches equal to the distance of 10cm. Place the measure vertically and count the number of rows, these should equal the tension given in the pattern.
If you have too many stitches to 10cm, try again using a thicker needle, if you have too few stitches to 10cm use a finer needle.
Note: Check your tension regularly as you knit, once you become relaxed and confident with your knitting, your tension can change.

Back

This is the start of your pattern. Following the colour code for your chosen size, you will be instructed how many stitches to cast on and to work from chart and written instructions as follows:

Knitting from charts

Each square on a chart represents one stitch; each line of squares indicates a row of knitting. When working from the chart, read odd numbered rows (right side of fabric) from right to left and even numbered rows (wrong side of fabric) from left to right.

Front (Fronts) and Sleeves

The pattern continues with instructions to make these garment pieces.

Pressing

Once you have finished knitting and before you begin to complete the garment it is important that all pieces are pressed, see page 48 for more details.

Neckband (Front bands)

This instruction tells you how to work any finishing off needed to complete your garment, such as knitting a neckband on a sweater or edgings on a cardigan. Once you have completed all the knitting you can begin to make up your garment, see page 48 for making up instructions.

Abbreviations

In the pattern you will find some of the most common words used have been abbreviated:

K	knit
P	purl
st(s)	stitches
inc	increase(e)(ing) knit into the front and back of next st to make 2 stitches.
dec	decreas(e)(ing)
st st	stocking stitch (right side row knit, wrong side row purl)
garter st	garter stitch (knit every row)
beg	begin(ning)
foll	follow(ing)
rem	remain(ing)
rev	reverse(ing)
rep	repeat
alt	alternate
cont	continue
patt	pattern
tog	together
cm	centimetres
in(s)	inch(es)
RS	right side
WS	wrong side
K2tog	knit two sts together to make one stitch
tbl	through back of loop
yo	yarn over, bring yarn over needle before working next st to create an extra loop.
M1	make one stitch by picking up horizontal loop before next stitch and knitting into back of it.
M1P	make one stitch by picking up horizontal loop before next stitch and purling into back of it.
CN	cable needle
C4B	slip next 2 sts onto CN, hold at back, K2, K2 from CN.
C4F	slip next 2 sts onto CN, hold at front, K2, K2 from CN.
C6B	slip next 3 sts onto CN, hold at back, K3, K3 from CN.
C6F	slip next 3 sts onto CN, hold at front, K3, K3 from CN.
C10B	slip next 5 sts onto CN, hold at back, K5, K5 from CN.

Knitting Techniques
A simple learn to knit guide

Introduction

Using illustrations and simple written instructions we have put together a beginners guide to knitting. With a basic knowledge of the simplest stitches you can create your own unique handknitted garments.

When you begin to knit you feel very clumsy, all fingers and thumbs. This stage passes as confidence and experience grows. Many people are put off hand knitting thinking that they are not using the correct techniques of holding needles, yarn or working of stitches, all knitters develop their own style, so please persevere.

Casting On

This is the term used for making a row of stitches; the foundation row for each piece of knitting. Make a slip knot. Slip this onto a needle. This is the basis of the two casting on techniques as shown below.

Thumb Cast On

This method uses only one needle and gives a neat, but elastic edge. Make a slip knot 1 metre from the cut end of the yarn, you use this length to cast on the stitches. For a knitted piece, the length between cut end and slip knot can be difficult to judge, allow approx 3 times the width measurement.

     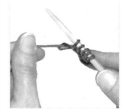

1. Make a slip knot approx 1 metre from the end of the yarn, with ball of yarn to your right.

2. Hold needle in RH. With the cut end of yarn held in LH, wrap yarn around your thumb from left to right anti-clockwise to front.

3. Insert RH needle into yarn around thumb, take yarn attached to ball around the back of RH needle to front.

4. Draw through needle to make a loop.

5. Pull on both ends of yarn gently. Creating a stitch on right hand needle.

6. Repeat from 2. until the required number of stitches has been cast on.

Cable Cast On

This method uses two needles; it gives a firm neat finish. It is important that you achieve an even cast on, this may require practice.

1. With slip knot on LH needle, insert RH needle. Take yarn behind RH needle; bring yarn forward between needles.

2. Draw the RH needle back through the slip knot, making a loop on RH needle with yarn.

3. Slip this loop onto left hand needle; taking care not to pull the loop too tight.

4. Insert the RH needle between the two loops on LH needle. Take yarn behind RH needle; bring yarn forward, between needles.

5. Draw through the RH needle making a loop as before. Slip this stitch onto LH needle.

6. Repeat from 4. until the required number of stitches has been cast on.

How to Knit -
The knit stitch is the simplest to learn. By knitting every row you create garter stitch and the simplest of all knitted fabrics.

    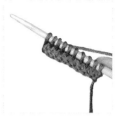

1. Hold the needle with the cast-on stitches in LH. Insert RH needle into first stitch.

2. Take yarn around the back of RH needle, bring yarn forward between needles.

3. Draw the RH needle through the stitch. Drop loop on LH needle

4. Making a loop on RH needle with yarn. One stitch made.

5. Repeat to the end of the row.

How to Purl -
The purl stitch is a little more complicated to master. Using a combination of knit and purl stitches together forms the bases of most knitted fabrics. The most common fabric knitted is stocking stitch, this is created when you knit 1 row, then purl 1 row.

1. Hold the needle with stitches on in LH and with yarn at the front of work, insert RH needle into front of stitch.

2. Take yarn around the back of RH needle, bring yarn to front.

3. Draw the needle through from front to back, making a loop on RH needle.

4. Slip the stitch onto right hand needle. Drop loop on LH needle.

5. Repeat to the end of the row.

Joining in a new yarn -
A new ball of yarn can be joined in on either a right side or a wrong side row, but to give a neat finish it is important you do this at the start of a row. Simply drop the old yarn, start knitting with the new ball, then after a few stitches tie the two ends together in a temporary knot. These ends are then sewn into the knitting at the making up stage, see page 48.

Casting Off -
This is the method of securing stitches at the top of your knitted fabric. It is important that the cast off edge should be elastic like the rest of the fabric; if you find that your cast off is too tight, try using a larger needle. You can cast off knitwise (as illustrated), purlwise, or in a combination of stitches, such as rib.

1. Hold the needle with the stitches on in LH, knit the first stitch.

2. Knit the next stitch from LH needle, two stitches on RH needle.

3. Using the point of LH needle; insert into first stitch on RH needle.

4. Take the first stitch over the second stitch.

5. One stitch on right hand needle.

6. Rep from 2. until one stitch on RH needle. Cut yarn, draw cut end through last stitch to secure.

Knitting Cables

Cables are used to add texture and pattern to your knitting. All the designs in 'Miss Bea's Rainy Day' use the same cabling technique. A separate double pointed cable needle is used to hold one set of stitches in front or behind your work, while the following group are knitted. When knitted on a plain background this resembles a rope. Combinations of using this very simple technique can create different patterns, in this book cables have been used to add interest to garment edgings, as central panels and as an all over fabric. The technique can be awkward at first but persevere as the effect is very rewarding.

C4B – Cable 4 back

Slip 2 sts onto cable needle and hold at back of work, knit next 2 sts from left-hand needle, then knit 2 sts from cable needle.

C4F – Cable 4 front

Slip 2 sts onto cable needle and hold at front of work, knit next 2 sts from left-hand needle, then knit 2 sts from cable needle.

C6B – Cable 6 back
Slip 3 sts onto cable needle, hold at back of work, knit next 3 sts from left-hand needle, then knit 3 sts from cable needle.

C6F – Cable 6 front
Slip 3 sts onto cable needle, hold at front of work, knit next 3 sts from left-hand needle, then knit 3 sts from cable needle.

C10B – Cable 10 back
Slip 5 sts onto cable needle, hold at back of work, knit next 5 sts from left-hand needle, then knit 5 sts from cable needle.

Make 1 stitch

Some patterns will require you increase stitches in the middle of a row to compensate for the cables, as cables make the fabric tighter than stocking stitch, you do this by making a stitch in the middle of a row as follows:

M1 – make 1 stitch knitwise. Pick up the strand of yarn lying between last stitch worked and next stitch and knit into the back of it.

M1P – make 1 stitch purlwise. Pick up the strand of yarn lying between last stitch worked and next stitch and purl into the back of it.

Rainy Day Sweater

Age 1-2 years 2-3 years 3-4 years

	Size		
Back	33cm (13in) 30cm (11¾in)	37cm (14½in) 31cm (12¼in)	41cm (16¼in) 33cm (13in)
Front			

Size

Sleeve: 21.5cm (8½in)   24.5cm (9¾in)   27.5cm (10¾in)

Yarn
Rowan Handknit Cotton x 50g balls
Flame   5   6   6

Needles
1 pair 3 ¼ mm (US 3) needles for edging
1 pair 4mm (US 6) needles for main body

Tension
20 sts and 28 rows to 10cm measured over stocking
stitch using 4 mm (US 6) needles

Back
Using 3 ¼ mm (US 3) needles, cast on 66,74,82 sts
and work from chart and written instructions as folls:
Chart row 1: P1, K1 to end.
Chart row 2: K1, P1 to end.
Change to 4mm (US 6) needles and cont to work in st
st only as folls:
Chart row 3: Knit.
Chart row 4: Purl.
Work until chart row 34,36,40 completed.

Shape armhole
Cast off 6 sts at the beg next 2 rows. (54,62,70 sts)
Work until chart row 72,76,82 completed.
Shape shoulders and back neck
Cast off 4,5,6 sts at the beg next 2 rows.
Chart row 75,79,85: Cast off 4,5,6 sts, knit until 6,7,8
sts on RH needle, turn and leave rem sts on a holder.
Chart row 76,80,86: Cast off 3 sts, purl to end.
Cast off rem 3,4,5 sts.
Slip centre 26,28,30 sts onto a holder, rejoin yarn to
rem sts and knit to end. (10,12,14 sts)
Chart row 76,80,86: Cast off 4,5,6 sts, purl to end.
(6,7,8 sts)
Chart row 77,81,87: Cast off 3 sts, knit to end.
Cast off rem 3,4,5 sts.

Front
Work as for back until chart row 68,72,78 completed.
Shape front neck
Chart row 69,73,79: Knit 17,20,23 sts, turn and leave
rem sts on a holder.
Chart row 70,74,80: Cast off 4 sts, purl to end.
Dec 1 st at neck edge on next 2 rows.
(11,14,17 sts)
Shape Shoulder
Chart row 73,77,83: Cast off 4,5,6 sts at beg next row
and foll alt row.
Purl 1 row.
Cast off rem 3,4,5 sts.
Slip centre 20,22,24 sts onto a holder, rejoin yarn to
rem sts and knit to end. (17,20,23 sts)
Purl 1 row
Chart row 71,75,81: Cast off 4 sts, knit to end.
Dec 1 st at neck edge on next 2 rows. (11,14,17 sts)
Shape shoulder
Chart row 74,78,84: Cast off 4,5,6 sts at beg next row
and foll alt row.
Knit 1 row.
Cast off rem 3,4,5 sts.

Sleeves (both alike)
Using 3 ¼ mm (US 3) needles cast on 34,36,38 sts and
work from chart and written instructions as folls:
Chart row 1: K0,1,0, (P1, K1) 17,17,19 times, P0,1,0.
Chart row 2: P0,1,0, (K1, P1) 17,17,19 times, K0,1,0.
Change to 4 mm (US 6) needles and cont to work in st
st only as folls:
Work 2 rows in st st.
Chart row 5: Inc into first st, knit to last st, inc into
last st. (36,38,40 sts)
Chart row 6: Purl.

Cont in st st from chart, shaping sides by inc as
indicated to 54,56,60 sts.
Work without further shaping until chart row
50,58,66 completed.
Cast off.

Press all pieces as shown in making up instructions,
page 48.

Neckband
Join right shoulder seam using backstitch.
Using 3 ¼ mm (US 3) needles pick up and knit 10 sts
down left front neck, knit across 20,22,24 sts on
holder, pick up and knit 10 sts to shoulder and 3 sts
down right back neck, knit across 26,28,30 sts on
holder, pick up and knit 3 sts to shoulder. (72,76,80 sts)
Edging row 1 (WS): K1, P1 to end.
Edging row 2: P1, K1 to end.
Work 4 more rows in moss stitch
Cast off knitwise on WS.

Complete sweater as shown in making up
instructions, page 48.

Cable Edging
Using 4 mm (US 6) needles cast on 12 sts and work
from chart and written instructions as folls:
Edging row 1: K1, P1, K6, (P1, K1) twice
Edging row 2: (K1, P1) twice, K1, P6, K1.
Work 8 more rows in patt from chart.
Edging row 11: K1, P1, slip next 5 sts onto CN,
hold at back, (K1, P1) twice, K1, K5 from CN.
Edging row 12: P5, (K1,P1) 3 times, K1.
Work 8 more rows in patt from chart.
Edging row 21: K1, P1, slip next 5 sts onto CN,
hold at back, K5, (K1, P1) twice, K1 from CN.
Edging row 22: (K1, P1) twice, K1, P6, K1.
Work 8 more rows in patt from chart.
Rep the last 20 rows until cable edging fits neatly
without stretching around lower edge of garment.
Cast off.
Slip stitch the cast on and cast off edges neatly
together to form a circle, and then matching the
seam with the right side seam slip stitch the straight
side of the edging evenly into place around the lower
edge of the sweater.
Work two more lengths of edging each long enough
to fit around the lower edge of the sleeves.
Slip stitch cast on and cast off edges together and
matching the seams slip stitch the straight side of the
edging into place around lower edge of each sleeve.

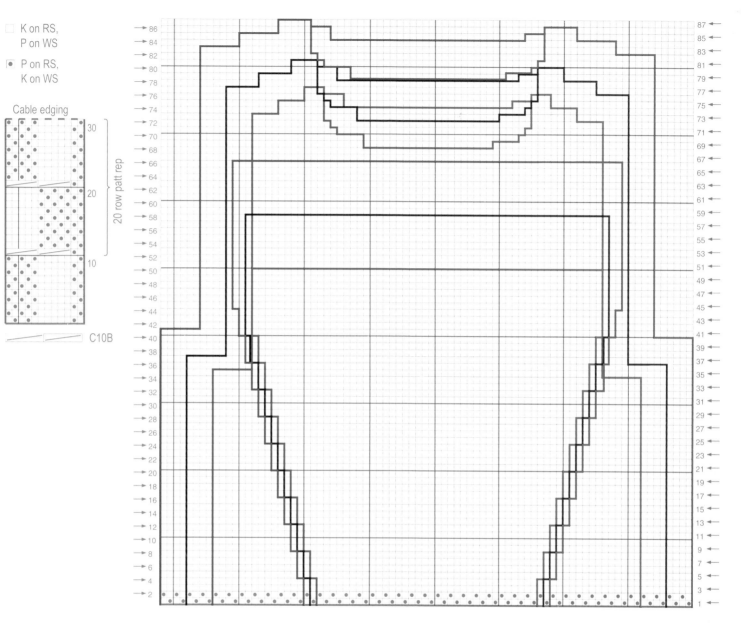

K on RS,
P on WS

P on RS,
K on WS

Cable edging

20 row patt rep

C10B

Bookworm Sweater

Age 1-2 years 2-3 years 3-4 years

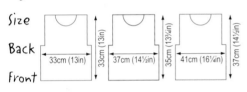

Size
Back
Front

Size
Sleeve

Yarn
Rowan All Seasons Cotton x 50g balls
True Blue   5   5   6

Needles
1 pair 4mm (US 6) needles for edging
1 pair 5mm (US 8) needles for main body

Tension
17 sts and 24 rows to 10cm measured over stocking stitch using 5mm (US 8) needles

Back
Using 4mm (US 6) needles cast on 61,67,73 sts and work from chart and written instructions as foll:
Chart row 1: P2,1,0, (K2, P2) 4,5,6 times, K6, P1, (K5, P1) twice, K6, (P2, K2) 4,5,6 times, P2,1,0.
Chart row 2: K2,1,0, (P2, K2) 4,5,6 times, P5, K1, P5, K1, P1, K1, P5, K1, P5, (K2, P2) 4,5,6 times, K2,1,0.
Chart row 3: P2,1,0, (K2, P2) 4,5,6 times, K4, (P1, K1) twice, (M1, K2) twice, P1, (K2, M1) twice, (K1, P1) twice, K4, (P2, K2) 4,5,6 times, P2,1,0. (65,71,77 sts)
Chart row 4: K2,1,0, (P2, K2) 4,5,6 times, P3, (K1, P1)

twice, P6, K1, P1, K1, P6, (P1, K1) twice, P3, (K2, P2) 4,5,6 times, K2,1,0.
Chart row 5: P2,1,0, (K2, P2) 4,5,6 times,K2, (P1, K1) twice, P1, C6B, K1, P1, K1, C6F, (P1, K1) twice, P1, K2, (P2, K2) 4,5,6 times, P2,1,0.
Chart row 6: Work as row 4.
Cont to work in rib cable patt from chart until row 10 completed.
Change to 5mm (US 8) needles and cont in patt from chart until chart row 50,52,54 completed.
Shape armhole
Cast off 5 sts at the beg next 2 rows. (55,61,67 sts)
Work until chart row 80,84,88 completed.
Shape back neck
Chart row 81,85,89: Patt until 15,17,19 sts on RH needle, turn and leave rem sts on a holder.
Chart row 82,86,90: Cast off 3 sts, patt to end.
Slip rem 12,14,16 sts onto a holder.
Slip centre 25,27,29 sts onto a holder, rejoin yarn to rem sts and patt to end. (15,17,19 sts)
Chart row 82,86,90: Patt 1 row.
Chart row 83,87,91: Cast off 3 sts, patt to end.
Slip rem 12,14,16 sts onto a holder.

Front
Work as for back to chart row 74,78,82 completed.
Shape front neck
Chart row 75,79,83: Patt 18,20,22 sts, turn and leave rem sts on a holder.
Chart row 76,80,84: Cast off 4 sts, patt to end.
Dec 1 st at neck edge on next 2 rows. (12,14,16 sts)
Work without further shaping until chart row 82,86,90 completed.
Slip rem sts onto a holder.
Slip centre 19,21,23 sts onto a holder, rejoin yarn to rem sts and patt to end. (18,20,22 sts)
Chart row 76,80,84: Patt 1 row.
Chart row 77,81,85: Cast off 4 sts, patt to end.
Dec 1 st at neck edge on next 2 rows. (12,14,16 sts)
Work without further shaping until chart row 83,87,91 completed. Slip rem sts onto a holder.

Sleeves (both alike)
Using 4mm (US 6) needles cast on 29,31,33 sts and work from chart and written instructions as folls:
Chart row 1: K0,1,2, P2, K6, P1, (K5, P1) twice, K6, P2, K0,1,2.
Chart row 2: P0,1,2, K2, P5, K1, P5, K1, P1, K1, P5, K1, P5, K2, P0,1,2.
Chart row 3: K0,1,2, P2, K4, (P1, K1) twice, (M1, K2) twice, P1, (K2, M1) twice, (K1, P1) twice, K4, P2, K0,1,2. (33,35,37 sts)

Chart row 4: P0,1,2, K2, P3, (K1, P1) twice, P6, K1, P1, K1, P6, (P1, K1) twice, P3, K2, P0,1,2.
Chart row 5: K0,1,2, P2, K2, (P1, K1) twice, P1, C6B, K1, P1, K1, C6F, (P1, K1) twice, P1, K2, P2, K0,1,2.
Chart row 6: Work as given for row 4.
Cont to work in rib cable patt from chart until row 10 completed.
Change to 5mm (US 8) needles and work in patt from chart as folls:
Chart row 11: Inc into first st, work in patt from chart to last st, inc into last st. (35,37,39 sts)
Chart row 12: Work in patt from chart.
Cont from chart, shaping sides by inc as indicated to 49,51,55 sts.
Work without further shaping until chart row 54,60,68 completed. Cast off.

Press all pieces as shown in making up instructions, page 48.

Neckband
Join right shoulder seam by knitting sts together on the RS of garment as shown in knitting techniques guide. With RS facing and using 4 mm (US 6) needles pick up and knit 10, sts down left front neck, patt across 19,21,23 sts on holder, pick up and knit 10 sts to shoulder and 3 sts down right back neck, patt across sts on holder as folls: K8,9,10, K2tog, (K2, K2tog) twice, K7,8,9, pick up and knit 3 sts to shoulder. (67,71,75 sts)
Edging row 1 (WS row): P0,2,0, (K2, P2) 10,10,11 times, K1, P7, K1, P1, K1, P7, K1, (P2, K2) 2,2,3 times, P0,2,0.
Edging row 2 (RS row): K0,2,0, (P2, K2) 2,2,3 times, K1, P1, C6B, K1, P1, K1, C6F, P1, K1, (P2, K2) 10,10,11 times, K0,2,0.
Edging row 3: Work as given for row 1.
Edging row 4: K0,2,0, (P2, K2) 2,2,3 times, K1, P1, K1, P1, K7, P1, K1, (P2, K2) 10,10,11 times, K0,2,0.
Rep the last 2 rows twice more.
Edging row 9: Work as given for row 1.
Edging row 10: Work as given for row 2.
Edging row 11: Work as given for row 1.
Edging row 12 (RS) (dec): K0,2,0, (P2, K2) 2,2,3 times, K1, P1, K2tog, K2, K2tog, K1, P1, K1, K2tog, K2, K2tog, P1, K1, (P2, K2) 10,10,11 times, K0,2,0. (63,67,71 sts)
Cast off in rib.
Join left shoulder seam by knitting sts together on the RS of garment as above. Join neckband seam using backstitch.
Complete sweater as shown on page 48.

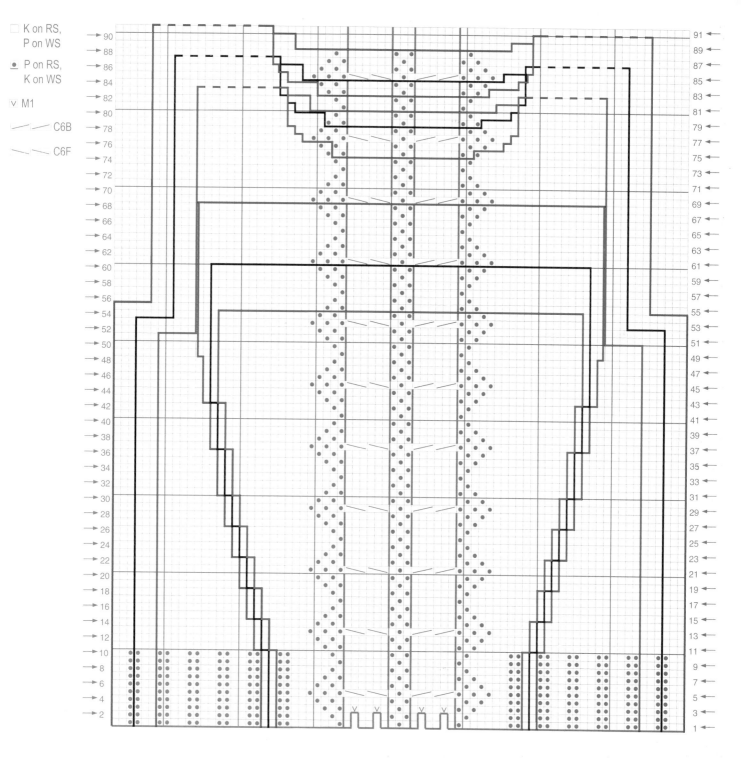

K on RS,
P on WS

● P on RS,
K on WS

∨ M1

C6B

C6F

31

Tower Cardigan

Age 1-2 years 2-3 years 3-4 years

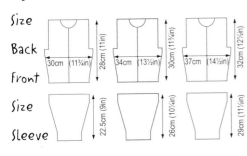

Size Back Front

30cm (11¾in) 28cm (11in)
34cm (13½in) 30cm (11¾in)
37cm (14½in) 32cm (12½in)

Size Sleeve

22.5cm (9in) 26cm (10¼in) 29cm (11½in)

Yarn
Rowan Wool Cotton x 50g balls
Mango   5   5   5

Needles
1 pair 3 ¼ mm (US 3) needles for edging
1 pair 4mm (US 6) needles for main body

Buttons 6,7,7

Tension
22 sts and 30 rows to 10cm measured over stocking
stitch using 4 mm (US 6) needles

Note The charts are for cardigan fronts only, Work
from written instructions for back and sleeves using chart
as a guide for back as shaping and rows are the same.

Left Front
Using 3 ¼ mm (US 3) needles cast on 30,34,37 sts and
work from chart and follow written instructions as folls:
Chart row 1: P1,1,0, (K1, P1) to last 7 sts, K7.
Chart row 2: K1, P7, (K1, P1) to last 0,0,1 st, K0,0,1.
Chart row 3: Work as given for row 1.

Chart row 4 (inc): K1,P1, (M1P, P2) 3 times, (K1, P1)
to last 0,0,1 st, K0,0,1. (33,37,40 sts)
Chart row 5: P1,1,0, (K1, P1) to last 10 sts, C6B, K4.
Chart row 6: K1, P10, (K1, P1) to last 0,0,1 st, K0,0,1.
Chart row 7: P1,1,0, (K1, P1) to last 10 sts, K3, C6F, K1.
Chart row 8: K1, P10, (K1, P1) to last 0,0,1 st, K0,0,1.
Rep the last 4 rows until chart row 16 completed.
Change to 4mm (US 6) needles and keeping cable
plait patt correct and working rem sts in st st cont from
chart as folls:
Chart row 17: Inc into first st, K to last 11 sts, P1, C6B,
K4. (34,38,41 sts)
Chart row 18: K1, P to end.
Cont from chart, shaping side edge by inc as indicated
to 37,41,44 sts.
Work until chart row 48,52,54 completed.
Shape armhole
Cast off 6 sts at the beg next row. (31,35,38 sts)
Cont until chart row 81,87,93 completed.
Shape front neck
Chart row 82,88,94: Cast off 1 st, (K2 tog, cast off 2 sts)
3 times, cast off 1,2,3 sts, purl to end. (20,23,25 sts)
Work 1 row.
Chart row 84,90,95: Cast off 4 sts, purl to end.
(16,19,21 sts)
Dec 1 st at neck edge on next 4 rows. (12,15,17 sts)
Shape shoulder
Cast off 4,5,6, sts at the beg next row and foll alt row.
Work 1 row.
Cast off rem 4,5,5 sts.

Right Front
Using 3 ¼ mm (US 3) needles cast on 30,34,37 sts and
work from chart and follow written instructions as folls:
Chart row 1: K7, (P1, K1) to last 1,1,0 st, P1,1,0.
Chart row 2: P1,1,0, (K1, P1) to last 7 sts, P6, K1.
Chart row 3: Work as given for row 1.
Chart row 4 (inc): P1,1,0, (K1, P1) to last 7 sts, P1,
(M1P, P2) twice, M1P, P1, K1. (33,37,40 sts)
Chart row 5: K4, C6F, (P1, K1) to last 1,1,0 st, P1,1,0.
Chart row 6: P1,1,0, (K1, P1) to last 10 sts, P9, K1.
Chart row 7: K1, C6B, K3, (P1, K1) to last 1,1,0 st,
P1,1,0.
Chart row 8: P1,1,0, (K1, P1) to last 10 sts, P9, K1.
Rep the last 4 rows until chart row 16 completed
Change to 4mm (US 6) needles, keeping cable plait patt
correct and working rem sts in st st, complete as for left
front foll chart for right front and reversing shaping.

Back
Using 3 ¼ mm (US 3) needles cast on 59,67,73 sts and
work from written instructions as folls:

Row 1: P1,1,0, (K1, P1) to last 0,0,1 st, K0,0,1.
Row 2: P1,1,0, (K1, P1) to last 0,0,1 st, K0,0,1.
Rep these 2 rows until 16 rows in all completed.
Change to 4mm (US 6) needles and beg with a K row
cont to work in st st **and at the same time** shape
sides as folls:
Inc 1 st at each end of next row and every foll 8th row
to 67,75,81 sts.
Work a further 7,11,13 rows, until 48,52,54 rows in all
completed.
Shape armhole
Cast off 6 sts at the beg next 2 rows. (55,63,69 sts)
Work until 88,94,100 rows in all completed.
Shape shoulders and back neck
Cast off 4,5,6, sts at the beg next 2 rows.
Row 91,97,103: Cast off 4,5,6 sts, patt until 7,8,8 sts
on RH needle, turn and leave rem sts on a holder.
Row 92,98,104: Cast off 3 sts, patt to end.
Cast off rem 4,5,5 sts.
Rejoin yarn and cast off centre 25,27,29 sts, patt to
end. (11,13,14 sts)
Row 92,98,104: Cast off 4,5,6 sts, patt to end. (7,8,8 sts)
Chart row 93,99,105: Cast off 3 sts, patt to end.
Cast off rem 4,5,5 sts.

Sleeves (both alike)
Using 3 ¼ mm (US 3) needles cast on 37,39,41 sts
and work from written instructions as folls:
Row 1: (K1, P1) to last st, K1.
Row 2: (K1, P1) to last st, K1.
Rep these 2 rows until 16 rows of moss st in all
completed.
Change to 4 mm (US 6) needles and beg with a K row,
cont in st st as folls:
Inc 1 st at each end of next row and every foll 4th row
to 49,51,53 sts.
Work 5 rows.
Inc 1 st at each end of next row and every foll 6th row
to 57,61,67 sts.
Work without further shaping until sleeve measures
22.5,26,29 cm from cast on edge. Cast off.

Press all pieces as shown on page 48.

Buttonhole band
With RS of right front facing and using 3 ¼ mm
(US 3) needles pick up and knit 57,63,67 sts from cast
on edge to start of neck shaping.
Buttonhole row: K1,0,1, P1, (yo, P2tog, (K1,P1) 4
times) 5,6,6 times, yo, P2tog, K1,0,1, P1,0,1, K1,0,1.
Next row: K1,0,1, (P1, K1) to last 0,1,0 st, P0,1,0.
Cast off knitwise.

eft front edging

With RS of left front facing and
using 3 ¼ mm (US 3) needles
pick up and knit 57,63,67 sts
from start of neck shaping to
cast on edge.
Work 2 rows in moss st.
Cast off knitwise.

Collar

Using 3 ¼ mm (US 3) needles
cast on 73,77,81 sts. Work
21,23,25 rows in moss st as
on sleeve, ending with a
WS row.
Cast off knitwise.
Join both shoulder seams
using backstitch.
Sew cast on edge of collar to
neck edge, matching row ends
at front opening edges.
Complete as shown on page 48.
Sew on buttons to correspond
with buttonholes.

	K on RS, P on WS
	P on RS, K on WS
V	Make 1P
	C6B
	C6F

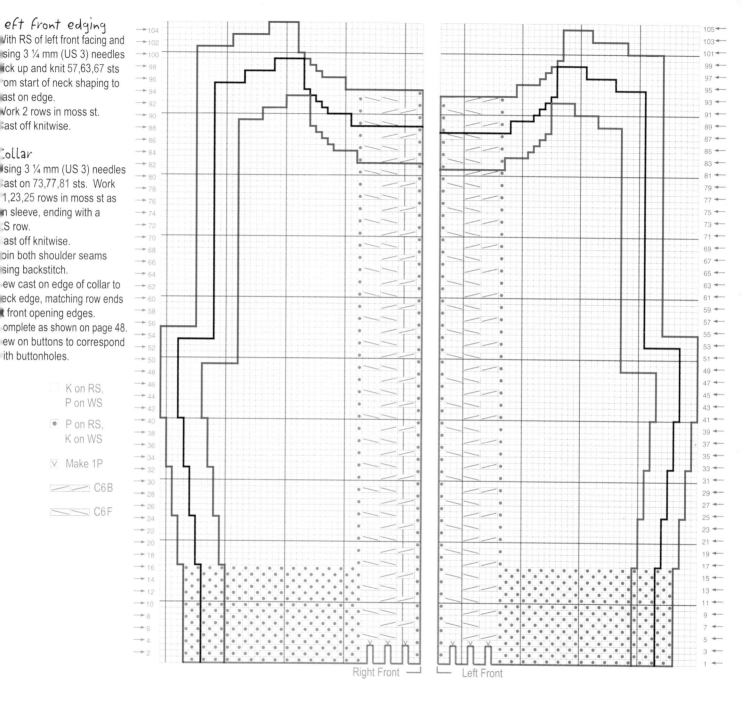

Right Front

Left Front

33

Train Track Slipover

Age 1-2 years   2-3 years   3-4 years

Size
Back
Front

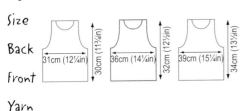

31cm (12¼in)   36cm (14¼in)   39cm (15¼in)
30cm (11¾in)   32cm (12½in)   34cm (13½in)

Yarn
Rowan Wool Cotton x 50g balls
Aqua   4   4   4

Needles
1 pair 3 ¼ mm (US 3) needles for edging
1 pair 4mm (US 6) needles for main body

Tension
24 sts and 30 rows to 10cm measured over cable
pattern using 4 mm (US 6) needles

Back
Using 3 ¼ mm (US 3) needles, cast on 62,72,80 sts
and work from chart and written instructions as folls:
Chart row 1: Knit.
Chart row 2: Purl.
Work these 2 rows once more.
Chart row 5: Knit.
Chart row 6 (inc): P4,4,8, (M1P, P5) 11,13,13 times,
M1P, P3,3,7. (74,86,94 sts)
Change to 4mm (US 6) needles and cont to work in
cable patt as folls:
Chart row 7: K0,0,4, (P2, K4) 12,14,14 times, P2,
K0,0,4.
Chart row 8: P0,0,4, (K2, P4) 12,14,14 times, K2,
P0,0,4.

Chart row 9: K0,0,4, P0,2,2, K0,4,4, (P2, C4B, P2, K4)
6 times, P2, (C4B, P2) 0,1,1 time, K0,0,4.
Chart row 10: Work as given for row 8.
Cont to work in cable patt as indicted on chart until row
58,62,66 completed.
Shape armhole
Cast off 6 sts at beginning next 2 rows. (62,74,82 sts)
Dec 1 st at each end of next 3 rows and 2 foll alt rows.
(52,64,72 sts)
Work 3 rows in patt.
Dec 1 st at each end of next row. (50,62,70 sts)
Work without further shaping to chart row 94,100,106
completed.
Shape shoulders and back neck
Cast off 4,6,7 sts at the beg next row, patt until 6,9,11
sts on RH needle, turn and leave rem sts on a holder.
Chart row 96,102,108: Cast off 3 sts, patt to end.
Cast off rem 3,6,8 sts.
Slip centre 30,32,34 sts onto a holder, rejoin yarn to
rem sts and patt to end. (10,15,18 sts)
Chart row 96,102,108: Cast off 4,6,7 sts, patt to end.
(6,9,11 sts)
Chart row 97,103,109: Cast off 3 sts, patt to end.
Cast off rem 3,6,8 sts.

Front
Work as for back until chart row 88,94,100 completed.
Shape front neck
Chart row 89,95,101: Patt 13,18,21 sts, turn and leave
rem sts on a holder.
Chart row 90,96,102: Cast off 4 sts, patt to end.
Dec 1 st at neck edge on next 2 rows. (7,12,15 sts)
Work 2 rows.
Shape Shoulder
Chart row 95,101,107: Cast off 4,6,7 sts at beg
next row.
Patt 1 row.
Cast off rem 3,6,8 sts.
Slip centre 24,26,28 sts onto a holder, rejoin yarn to
rem sts and patt to end. (13,18,21 sts)
Patt 1 row
Chart row 91,97,103: Cast off 4 sts, patt to end.
Dec 1 st at neck edge on next 2 rows. (7,12,15 sts)
Work 2 rows.
Shape shoulder
Chart row 96,102,108: Cast off 4,6,7 sts at beg
next row.   Patt 1 row.
Cast off rem 3,6,8 sts.

Press all pieces as shown in making up instructions,
page 48.

Neck Edging
Join right shoulder seam using backstitch.
With RS facing and using 3 ¼ mm (US 3) needles
pick up and knit 10 sts down left front neck, patt
across 24,26,28 sts on front neck holder as folls:
K2,3,4, (K2 tog, K4) 3 times, K2tog, K2,3,4 pick up
and knit 10 sts to shoulder and 3 sts down right back
neck, patt across 30,32,34 sts on back neck holder
as folls: K5,6,7, (K2 tog, K4) 3 times, K2tog, K5,6,7,
pick up and knit 3 sts to shoulder. (72,76,80 sts)
Beg with a P row work 7 rows in st st.
Cast off knitwise.
Join left shoulder seam and neckband using backstitch.

Armhole edging (both alike)
With RS facing and using 3 ¼ mm (US 3) needles
and RS of garment facing pick up and knit 34,36,38 sts
from side seam to shoulder and 34,36,38 sts down to
side seam. (68,72,76 sts)
Knit 2 rows.
Cast off knitwise.
Complete slipover as shown in making up instructions,
page 48.

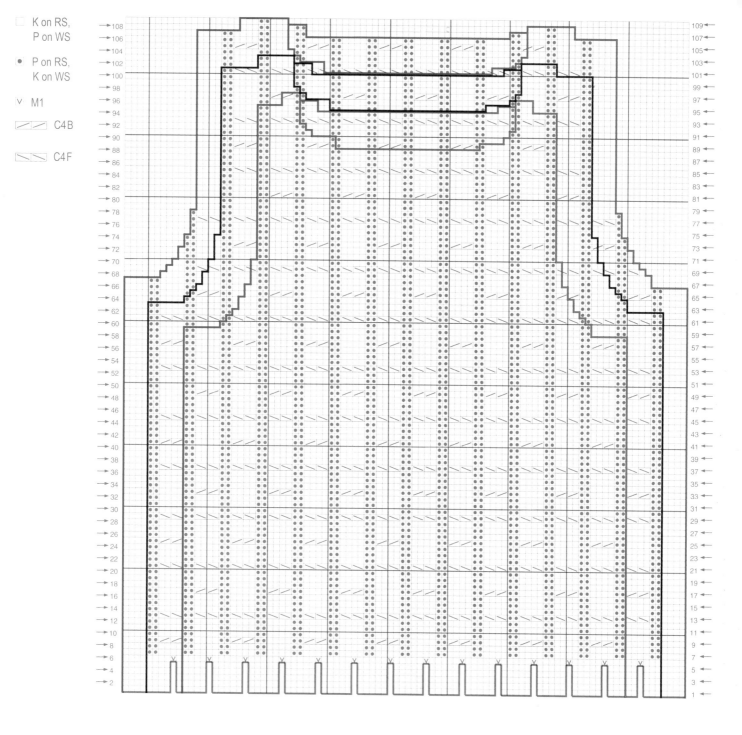

Smiling Jacket

Age 1-2 years · 2-3 years · 3-4 years

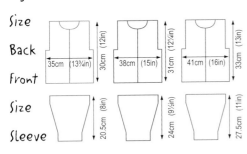

Yarn
Rowan Handknit Cotton x 50g balls
Diana 6 6 6

Needles
1 pair 3 ¼ mm (US 3) needles for edging
1 pair 4mm (US 6) needles for main body

Zip
Open-ended zip to fit

Tension
20 sts and 28 rows to 10cm measured over stocking stitch using 4 mm (US 6) needles

Back
Using 3 ¼ mm (US 3) needles cast on 70,76,82 sts and work from chart A and written instructions as folls:
Chart row 1: Knit.
Chart row 2: P0,2,5, K1,2,2, (P5, K2) 9 times, P5, K1,2,2, P0,2,5.
Chart row 3 (inc): K4,7,10, (M1, K7) 9 times, M1, K3,6,9. (80,86,92 sts)
Chart row 4: P0,2,5, K1,2,2, (P6, K2) 9 times, P6, K1,2,2, P0,2,5.

Change to 4 mm (US 6) needles and cont to work from chart for cable edging as follows:
Chart row 5: K1,4,7, (C6B, K2) 9 times, C6B, K1,4,7.
Chart row 6: Work as given for row 4.
Cont to work from chart for cable patt until chart row 22 completed.
Chart row 23 (dec): K3,6,9, (K2tog, K6) 9 times, K2tog, K3,6,9. (70,76,82 sts)
Chart row 24: Work as given for row 2.
Cont to work in st st from chart B as folls:
Chart row 25: Knit.
Chart row 26: Purl.
Work until chart row 48,48,52 completed.
Shape armhole
Cast off 6 sts at the beg next 2 rows. (58,64,70 sts)
Work until chart row 84,86,92 completed.
Shape back neck
Chart row 85,87,93: Patt until 18,20,22 sts on RH needle, turn and leave rem sts on a holder.
Chart row 86,88,94: Cast off 3 sts, patt to end.
Slip rem 15,17,19 sts onto a holder.
Rejoin yarn and cast off centre 22,24,26 sts, knit to end. (18,20,22 sts)
Chart row 86,88,94: Patt 1 row.
Chart row 87,89,95: Cast off 3 sts, patt to end.
Slip rem 15,17,19 sts onto a holder.

Left front
Using 3 ¼ mm (US 3) needles cast on 36,39,42 sts and work from chart A and written instructions as folls:
Chart row 1: Knit.
Chart row 2: (K2, P5) 5 times, K1,2,2, P0,2,5.
Chart row 3 (inc): K4,6,10, (M1, K7) 4 times, M1, K4. (41,44,47 sts)
Chart row 4: (K2, P6) 5 times, K1,2,2, P0,2,5.
Change to 4 mm (US 6) needles and cont to work from chart for cable edging as follows:
Chart row 5: K1,4,7, (C6B, K2) 5 times.
Chart row 6: Work as given for row 4.
Cont to work from chart for cable patt until chart row 22 completed.
Note: The cable patt at centre front conts throughout, from this point these 10 sts are **not** shown on chart.
Chart row 23 (dec): K3,6,9, (K2tog, K6) 3 times, K2tog, K12. (37,40,43 sts)
Chart row 24: K2, P6, (K2, P5) 4 times, K1,2,2,P0,2,5.
Cont from chart B, keeping cable patt correct over the 10 sts at centre front and rem sts in st st, work until chart row 48,48,52 completed.
Shape armhole
Cast off 6 sts at the beg next row. (31,34,37 sts)
Work until chart row 77,79,85 completed.

Shape front neck
Chart row 78,80,86: Patt 10 sts and slip these onto a holder, purl to end. (21,24,27 sts)
Work 1 row.
Chart row 80,82,88: Cast off 4,5,6 sts, purl to end. Dec 1 st at neck edge on next 2 rows. (15,17,19 sts)
Work without further shaping until chart row 86,88,94 completed. Slip rem sts onto a holder

Right Front
Using 3 ¼ mm (US 3) needles cast on 36,39,42 sts and work from chart A and written instructions as folls:
Chart row 1: Knit.
Chart row 2: P0,2,5, K1,2,2, (P5, K2) 5 times.
Chart row 3 (inc): K5, (M1, K7) 4 times, M1, K3,6,9. (41,44,47 sts)
Chart row 4: P0,2,5, K1,2,2,(P6, K2) 5 times.
Change to 4 mm (US 6) needles and cont to work from chart for cable edging as follows:
Chart row 5: (K2, C6B) 5 times, K1,4,7.
Chart row 6: Work as given for row 4.
Cont to work from chart for cable patt until chart row 22 completed.
Note: The cable patt at centre front conts throughout, from this point these 10 sts are **not** shown on chart.
Chart row 23 (dec): K12, (K2tog, K6) 3 times, K2tog, K3,6,9. (37,40,43 sts)
Chart row 24: P0,2,5, K1,2,2, (P5, K2) 4 times, P6, K2.
Cont from chart B, keeping cable patt correct over the 10 sts at centre front and rem sts in st st, work until chart row 49,49,53 completed.
Complete to match left front, foll chart for right front.

Sleeves (both alike)
Using 3 ¼ mm (US 3) needles cast on 34,36,38 sts and work from chart C and written instructions as folls
Chart row 1: Knit.
Chart row 2: P2,3,4, (K2, P5) 4 times, K2, P2,3,4.
Chart row 3 (inc): K7,8,9, (M1, K7) 3 times, M1, K6,7,8. (38,40,42 sts)
Chart row 4: P2,3,4, (K2, P6) 4 times, K2, P2,3,4.
Change to 4 mm (US 6) needles and cont to work from chart for cable edging as follows:
Chart row 5: K4,5,6, (C6B, K2) 4 times, K2,3,4.
Chart row 6: Work as given for row 4.
Cont to work from chart for cable patt until chart row 10 completed.
Chart row 11(inc): Inc into first st, knit to last st, Inc into last st. (40,42,44 sts)
Chart row 12: P3,4,5, (K2, P6) 4 times, K2, P3,4,5.
Keeping cable patt correct, cont until chart row 22 completed and **at the same time** shape sides by inc

as indicated. (44,46,48 sts)

Chart row 23 (dec): Inc into first st, K8,9,10, (K2tog, K6) 4 times, K2,3,4, inc into last st. (42,44,46 sts)

Chart row 24: P6,7,8, (K2, P5) 4 times, K2, P6,7,8.

Work 2 rows in st st from chart B.

Chart row 27 Inc into first st, knit to last st, inc into last st. (44,46,48 sts)

Chart row 28: Purl.

Cont in st st from chart, shaping sides by inc as indicated to 54,56,60 sts.

Work without further shaping until chart row 60,70,80 completed. Cast off.

Press all pieces as shown in instructions on page 48.

Neckband

Join both shoulder seams by knitting sts together on WS of garment as shown on page 48.

With RS facing and using 3 ¼ mm (US 3) needles knit across 10 sts from holder, pick up and knit 10,11,12, sts up right front neck shaping, 28,30,32 sts across back neck, 10,11,12 sts down left front neck, and knit across 10 sts from holder. (68,72,76 sts)

Row 1(WS): K2, P6, K2, purl to last 10 sts, K2, P6, K2.

Row 2: K2, C6B, knit to last 8 sts, C6B, K2.

Row 3: Work as given for row 1.

Row 4: Knit.

Row 5: Work as given for row 1.

Work the last 4 rows once more.

Next row (RS)(dec): K3, K2tog twice, knit to last 7 sts, K2tog twice, K3.

Knit 2 rows. Cast off knitwise.

Complete Jacket as shown on page 48.

☐ K on RS,
    P on WS

• P on RS,
    K on WS

▽ M1

⊼ K2 tog

⟋⟋ C6B

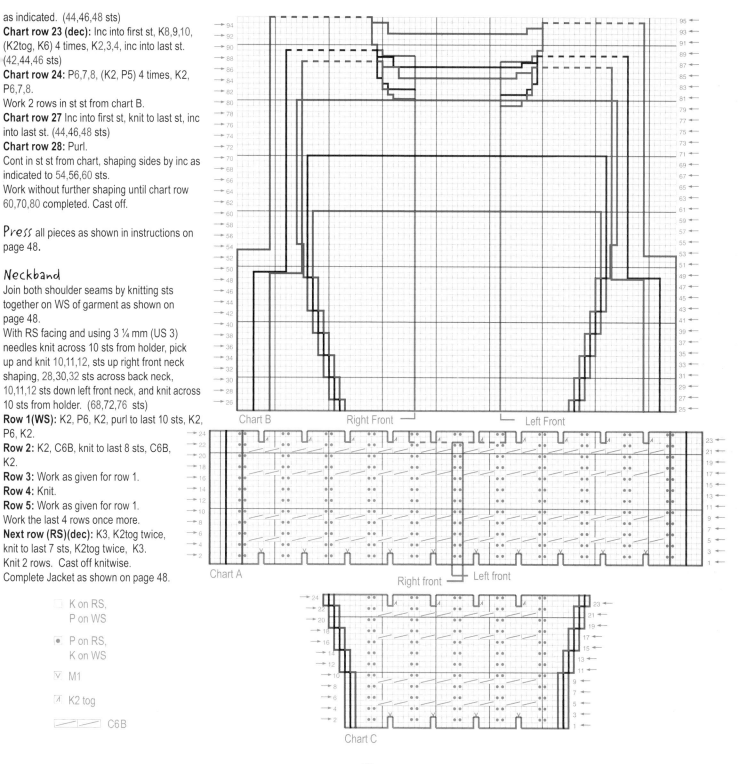

37

Racing Sweater

Age 1-2 years   2-3years   3-4 years

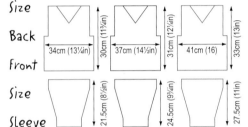

Size Back — 34cm (13¼in) / 30cm (11¾in) / 37cm (14½in) / 31cm (12¼in) / 41cm (16) / 33cm (13in)

Size Front

Size Sleeve — 21.5cm (8½in) / 24.5cm (9¾in) / 27.5cm (11in)

Yarn
Rowan Handknit Cotton x 50g balls
Gooseberry   5   6   6

Needles
1 pair 3 ¼ mm (US 3) needles for rib
1 pair 4mm (US 6) needles for main body

Tension
20 sts and 28 rows to 10cm measured over stocking stitch using 4 mm (US 6) needles

Back
Using 3 ¼ mm (US 3) needles, cast on 68,74,82 sts and work from chart and written instructions as folls:
Chart row 1: K0,3,7, (P1, K3, P1, K4) 7 times, P1, K3, P1, K0,3,7.
Chart row 2: P0,3,7, (K1, P3, K1, P4) 7 times, K1, P3, K1, P0,3,7.
Chart row 3: K0,3,7, (P1, K2, M1, K1, P1, K4) 7 times, P1, K2, M1, K1, P1, K0,3,7. (76,82,90 sts)
Chart row 4: P0,3,7, (K1 P4), 15 times, K1, P0,3,7.
Chart row 5: K0,3,7, (P1, C4B, P1, K4) 7 times, P1, C4B, P1, K0,3,7.

Chart row 6: Work as given for row 4.
Cont in cable rib from chart until row 18 completed.
Chart row 19: K0,3,7, (P1, K1, K2tog, K1, P1, K4) 7 times, P1, K1, K2tog, K1, P1, K0,3,7. (68,74,82 sts)
Chart row 20: Work as given for row 2.
Change to 4mm (US 6) needles and cont in st st as folls:
Chart row 21: Knit.
Chart row 22: Purl.
Work until chart row 48,48,52 completed.

Shape armhole
Cast off 6 sts at the beg next 2 rows. (56,62,70 sts)
Work until chart row 86,88,94 completed.

Shape shoulders and back neck
Cast off 5,5,6 sts at the beg next 2 rows.
Chart row 89,91,97: Cast off 5,5,6 sts, knit until 7,9,10 sts on RH needle, turn and leave rem sts on a holder.
Chart row 90,92,98: Cast off 3 sts, purl to end.
Cast off rem 4,6,7 sts.
Slip centre 22,24,26 sts onto a holder, rejoin yarn to rem sts and knit to end. (12,14,16 sts)
Chart row 90,92,98: Cast off 5,5,6 sts, purl to end. (7,9,10 sts)
Chart row 91,93,99: Cast off 3 sts, knit to end.
Cast off rem 4,6,7 sts.

Front
Work as for back until chart row 54,56,60 completed. (56,62,70 sts)

Shape front neck
Chart row 55,57,61: Knit 27,30,34 sts, turn and leave rem 29,32,36 sts on a holder.
Work 1 row.
Chart row 57,59,63: Knit to last 2 sts, K2tog.
Work 1 row.
Cont to dec as indicated at front neck until 14,16,19 sts rem.
Work until chart row 86,88,94 completed.

Shape Shoulder
Chart row 87,89,95: Cast off 5,5,6 sts at beg next row and foll alt row. Work 1 row.
Cast off rem 4,6,7 sts.
Slip centre 2 sts onto a holder, rejoin yarn to rem sts and knit to end. (27,30,34 sts)
Work 1 row.
Chart row 57,59,63: K2tog, knit to end. Work 1 row.
Cont to dec as indicated at front neck until 14,16,19 sts rem.
Work until chart row 87,89,95 completed.

Shape shoulder
Chart row 88,90,96: Cast off 5,5,6 sts at beg next row and foll alt row. Work 1 row.
Cast off rem 4,6,7 sts.

Sleeves (both alike)
Using 3 ¼ mm (US 3) needles cast on 34,36,38 sts and work from chart and written instructions as folls:
Chart row 1: K1,2,3, (P1, K3, P1, K4) 3 times, P1, K3, P1, K1,2,3.
Chart row 2: P1,2,3, (K1, P3, K1, P4) 3 times, K1, P3, K1, P1,2,3.
Chart row 3: K1,2,3, (P1, K2, M1, K1, P1, K4) 3 times, P1, K2, M1, K1, P1, K1,2,3. (38,40,42 sts)
Chart row 4: P1,2,3, (K1, P4) 7 times, K1, P1,2,3.
Chart row 5: K1,2,3, (P1, C4B, P1, K4) 3 times, P1, C4B, P1, K1,2,3.
Chart row 6: Work as given for row 4.
Cont in cable rib from chart until row 18 completed.
Chart row 19: K1,2,3, (P1, K1, K2tog, K1, P1, K4) 3 times, P1, K1, K2tog, K1, P1, K1,2,3. (34,36,38 sts)
Chart row 20: Work as given for row 2.
Change to 4mm (US 6) needles and cont in st st as foll:
Chart row 21: Inc into first st, knit to last st, inc into last st. (36,38,40 sts)
Chart row 22: Purl.
Cont in from chart, shaping sides by inc as indicated to 54,56,60 sts.
Work without further shaping until chart row 62,70,80 completed.
Cast off.

Press all pieces as shown in making up instructions, page 48.

Neckband
Join right shoulder seam using backstitch.
With RS facing and using 3 ¼ mm (US 3) needles pick up and knit 30,31,32 sts down left front neck, knit across 2 sts on holder, pick up and knit 30,31,32 sts to shoulder and 3 sts down right back neck, pick up and knit across 22,24,26, sts at centre back, pick up and knit 3 sts to shoulder. (90,94,98 sts)
Edging row 1 (WS row): K57,60,63, K2tog, K2tog tbl, K29,30,31.
Edging row 2 (RS row): K28,29,30, K2tog tbl, K2tog, K56,59,62.
Edging row 3: K55,58,61, K2tog, K2tog tbl, K27,28,29.
Edging row 4: K26,27,28, K2tog tbl, K2tog, K54,57,60.
Edging row 5: K53,56,59, K2tog, K2tog tbl, K25,26,27.
Edging row 6: K24,25,26, K2tog tbl, K2tog, K52,55,58.
Cast off 51,54,57 sts knitwise, K2tog, cast off, K2tog tbl, cast off cast off rem sts knitwise
Join left shoulder seam and neckband using backstitch.
Complete sweater as shown in making up instructions, page 48.

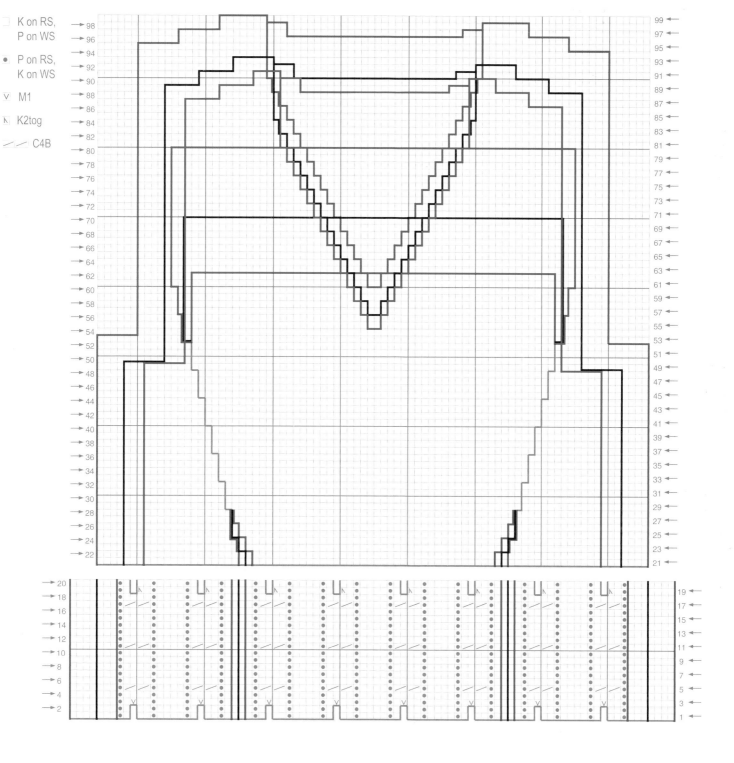

K on RS,
P on WS

• P on RS,
K on WS

v M1

K2tog

C4B

39

Cookie Sweater

Age 1-2 years 2-3 years 3-4 years

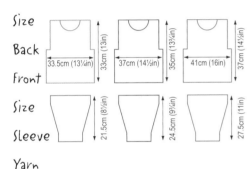

Size

Back

33.5cm (13¼in)   33cm (13in)

37cm (14½in)   35cm (13¾in)

41cm (16in)   37cm (14½in)

Front

Size

Sleeve

21.5cm (8½in)   24.5cm (9¾in)   27.5cm (11in)

Yarn
Rowan All Seasons x 50g balls

Red   4   5   5

Needles
1 pair 4mm (US 6) needles for ribs
1 pair 5mm (US 8) needles for main body

Tension
17 sts and 24 rows to 10cm measured over stocking stitch using 5mm (US 8) needles

Back
Using 4 mm (US 6) needles, cast on 57,63,69 sts and work from chart A and written instructions as folls:
Chart row 1: K0,3,1, (P2, K3) 11,12,13 times, P2,0,2, K0,0,1.
Chart row 2: P0,0,1, K2,0,2, (P3, K2) 11,12,13 times, P0,3,1.
Cont in rib until chart row 12 completed.
Change to 5mm (US 8) needles and work in patt setting sts as folls:

Chart row 13: Knit
Chart row 14: P4,1,4, (K1,P5) 8,10,10 times, K1, P4,1,4.
Cont to work from chart until row 50,52,54 completed.
Shape armhole
Cast off 5 sts at the beg next 2 rows. (47,53,59 sts)
Now work from chart B for yoke as folls:
Chart row 1: K0,3,6, *(P1, K2) twice, P1, K1, M1, K2, rep from * 3 times more, (P1, K2) twice. P1, K0,3,6. (51,57,63 sts)
Cont to work in yoke pattern until chart row 28,30,32 completed.
Shape shoulders and back neck
Chart row 29,31,33: Patt until 15,17,19 sts on RH needle, turn and leave rem sts on a holder.
Chart row 30,32,34: Cast off 3 sts, patt to end.
Slip rem 12,14,16 sts onto a holder.
Rejoin yarn to rem sts, cast off centre 21,23,25 sts, patt to end. (15,17,19 sts)
Work 1 row.
Chart row 31,33,35: Cast off 3 sts, patt to end.
Slip rem 12,14,16 sts onto a holder.

Front
Work as for back until row 22,24,26 of chart B completed.
Shape front neck
Chart row 23,25,27: Patt 18,20,22 sts, turn and leave rem sts on a holder.
Chart row 24,26,28: Cast off 4 sts, patt to end.
Dec 1 st at neck edge on next 2 rows. (12,14,16 sts)
Work without further shaping until chart row 30,32,34 completed.
Slip rem sts onto a holder.
Rejoin yarn to rem sts, cast off centre 15,17,19 sts, patt to end. (18,20,22 sts)
Patt 1 row
Chart row 25,27,29: Cast off 4 sts, patt to end.
Dec 1 st at neck edge on next 2 rows. (12,14,16 sts)
Work without further shaping until chart row 31,33,35 completed.
Slip rem sts onto a holder.

Sleeves (both alike)
Using 4 mm (US 6) needles cast on 29,31,33 sts and work from chart A and written instructions as folls:
Chart row 1: K1,2,3 (P2, K3) 5 times, P2, K1,2,3.
Chart row 2: P1,2,3 (K2, P3) 5 times, K2, P1,2,3.
Cont in rib until chart row 12 completed.
Change to 5 mm (US 8) needles and cont to work in patt as folls:
Chart row 13: Inc into first st, knit to last st, inc into last st. (31,33,35 sts)

Chart row 14: P3,4,5, (K1, P5) 4 times, K1, P3,4,5.
Cont in patt from chart, shaping sides by inc as indicated to 45,47,51 sts.
Work without further shaping until chart row 54,60,6 completed.
Cast off.

Press all pieces as shown in making up instruction page 48.

Neckband
Join right shoulder seam by knitting sts together on the RS of garment as shown in knitting techniques guide, page 48.
With RS facing and using 4 mm (US 6) needles pick up and knit 10, sts down left front neck, pick up and knit across 14,17,19 sts at centre front, pick up and knit 10 sts to shoulder and 3 sts down right back nec pick up and knit across 20,22,25 sts at centre back, pick up and knit 3 sts to shoulder. (60,65,70 sts)
Rib row 1 (WS row): K2, P3 to end.
Rib row 2 (RS row): K3, P2 to end.
Work these 2 rows 4 times more.
Cast off in rib.
Join left shoulder seam by knitting sts together on th RS of garment as above. Join neckband seam using backstitch.
Complete sweater as shown in making up instructions, page 48.

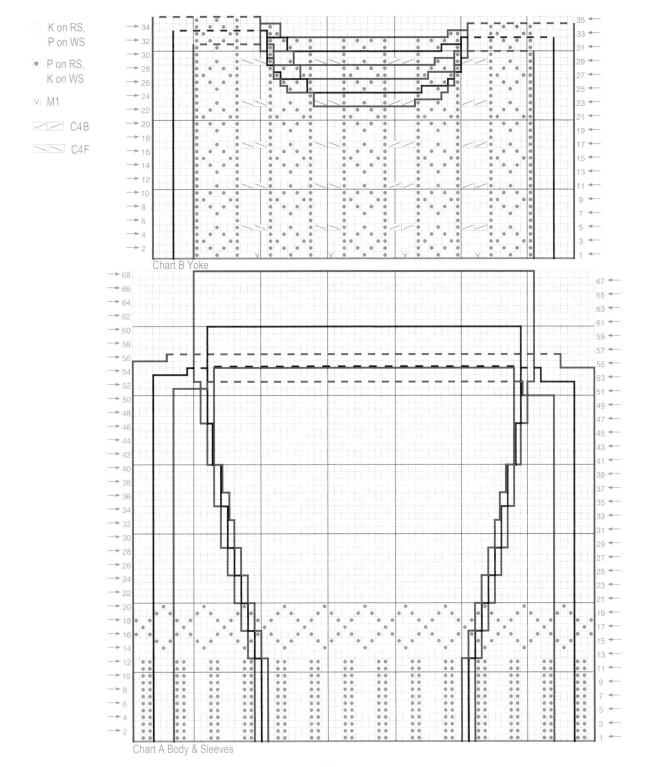

K on RS,
P on WS

● P on RS,
K on WS

v M1

C4B

C4F

Chart B Yoke

Chart A Body & Sleeves

41

Tea For Two Sweater

Age 1-2 years 2-3 years 3-4 years

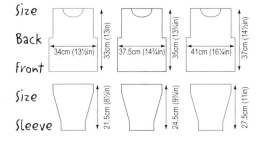

Size		
Back		
Front		

Back: 34cm (13½in) / 33cm (13in), 37.5cm (14¾in) / 35cm (13¾in), 41cm (16¼in) / 37cm (14¼in)

Size
Sleeve: 21.5cm (8½in), 24.5cm (9¾in), 27.5cm (11in)

Yarn
Rowan Handknit Cotton x 50g balls

Sugar	7	8	8

Needles
1 pair 3 ¼ mm (US 3) needles for rib
1 pair 4mm (US 6) needles for main body

Tension
24 sts and 28 rows to 10cm measured over cable pattern using 4 mm (US 6) needles

Back
Using 3 ¼ mm (US 3) needles, cast on 70,78,86 sts and work from chart and written instructions as folls:
Chart row 1: P2, K2 to last 2 sts, P2.
Chart row 2: K2, P2 to last 2 sts, K2.
Cont in rib from chart until row 15 completed.
Chart row 16: Patt 12,16,20, (M1P, patt 4, M1P, patt 10) 3 times, M1P, patt 4, M1P, patt 12,16,20. (78,86,94 sts)
Change to 4mm (US 6) needles and cont to work in patt setting sts as folls:
Chart row 17: K10,14,18, (P1, K8, P1, K6) 3 times, P1,

K 8, P1, K10,14,18.
Chart row 18: P10,14,18, (K1, P8, K1, P6) 3 times, K1, P8, K1, P10,14,18.
Chart row 19: K10,14,18, (P1, C4B, C4F, P1, K6) 3 times, P1, C4B, C4F, P1, K10,14,18.
Chart row 20: Work as given for chart row 18.
Work in cable patt from chart until row 58,60,64 completed.

Shape armhole
Cast off 6 sts at the beg next 2 rows. (66,74,82 sts)
Work until chart row 94,100,106 completed.

Shape shoulders and back neck
Cast off 5,5,6 sts at the beg next 2 rows.
Chart row 97,103,109: Cast off 5,5,6 sts, patt until 7,10,11 sts on RH needle, turn and leave rem sts on a holder.
Chart row 98,104,110: Cast off 3 sts, patt to end.
Cast off rem 4,7,8 sts.
Slip centre 32,34,36 sts onto a holder, rejoin yarn to rem sts and patt to end. (12,15,17 sts)
Chart row 98,104,110: Cast off 5,5,6 sts, patt to end. (7,10,11 sts)
Chart row 99,105,111: Cast off 3 sts, patt to end.
Cast off rem 4,7,8 sts.

Front
Work as for back until chart row 90,96,102 completed.

Shape front neck
Chart row 91,97,103: Patt 20,23,26 sts, turn and leave rem sts on a holder.
Chart row 92,98,104: Cast off 4 sts, patt to end.
Dec 1 st at neck edge on next 2 rows. (14,17,20 sts)

Shape Shoulder
Chart row 95,101,107: Cast off 5,5,6 sts at beg next row and foll alt row.
Patt 1 row.
Cast off rem 4,7,8 sts.
Slip centre 26,28,30 sts onto a holder, rejoin yarn to rem sts and patt to end. (20,23,26 sts)
Patt 1 row
Chart row 93,99,105: Cast off 4 sts, patt to end.
Dec 1 st at neck edge on next 2 rows. (14,17,20 sts)

Shape shoulder
Chart row 96,102,108: Cast off 5,5,6 sts at beg next row and foll alt row.
Patt 1 row.
Cast off rem 4,7,8 sts.

Sleeves (both alike)
Using 3 ¼ mm (US 3) needles cast on 34,36,38 sts and work from chart and written instructions as folls:
Chart row 1: P0,1,2, K2, P2 to last 2,3,4 sts, K2,

P0,1,2.
Chart row 2: K0,1,2, P2, K2 to last 2,3,4 sts, P2, K0,1,2.
Cont in rib from chart until row 15 completed
Chart row 16: Patt 8,9,10, M1P, patt 4, M1P, patt 10, M1P, patt 4, M1P, patt 8,9,10. (38,40,42 sts)
Change to 4mm (US 6) needles and cont to work in patt setting sts as foll:
Chart row 17: Inc into first st, P0,0,1, K5,6,6, P1, K8, P1, K6, P1, K8, P1, K5,6,6, P0,0,1, inc into last st. (40,42,44 sts)
Chart row 18: P0,1,2, (K1, P6, K1, P8) twice, K1, P6, K1, P0,1,2.
Chart row 19: Inc into first st, K0,0,1, P0,1,1, (K6, C4B, C4F, P1) twice, K6, P0,1,1, K0,0,1, inc into last st. (42,44,46 sts)
Chart row 20: P1,2,3, (K1, P6, K1, P8) twice, K1, P6, K1, P1,2,3.
Taking extra stitches into patt as soon as possible, cont in cable patt from chart, shaping sides by inc as indicated to 62,68,72 sts.
Work without further shaping until chart row 62,70,80 completed.
Cast off.

Press all pieces as shown in making up instructions, page 48.

Neckband
Join right shoulder seam using backstitch.
With RS facing and using 3 ¼ mm (US 3) needles pick up and knit 10, sts down left front neck, work across 26,28,30 sts on holder at front neck as folls: K2,3,4, K2tog, K2, K2tog, K10, K2tog, K2, K2tog, K2,3,4, pick up and knit 10 sts to shoulder and 3 sts down right back neck, work across 32,34,36 sts on holder at back neck as folls: K5,6,7, K2tog, K2, K2tog, K10, K2tog, K2, K2tog, K5,6,7, pick up and knit 3 sts to shoulder. (76,80,84 sts)
Rib row 1 (WS row): K2, P2 to end.
Rib row 2 (RS row): K2, P2 to end.
Work 9 more rows in rib.
Cast off in rib.
Join left shoulder seam and neckband using backstitch.
Complete sweater as shown in making up instructions, page 48, leaving 16 rows at bottom edge of garment open for side vent.

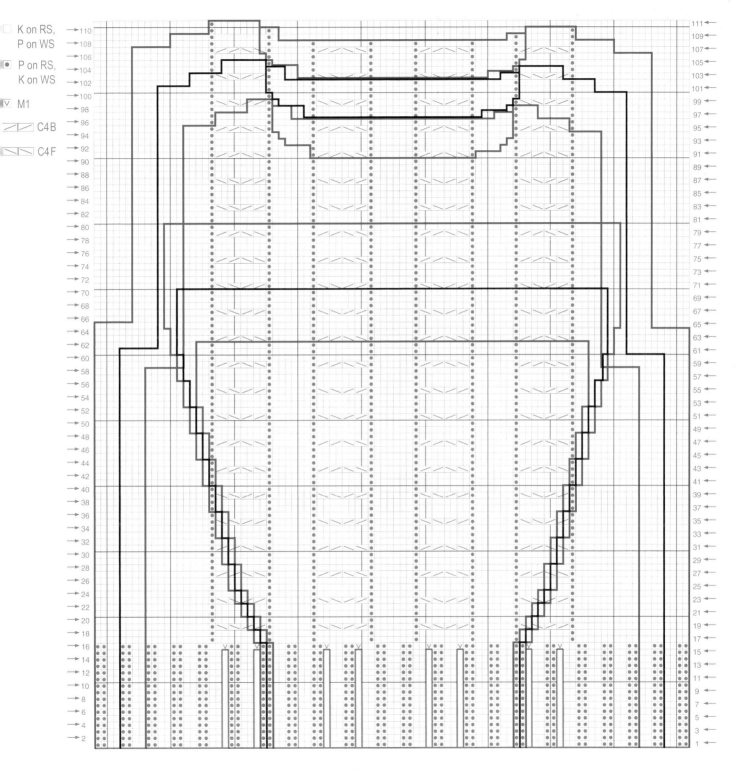

K on RS,
P on WS

P on RS,
K on WS

M1

C4B

C4F

43

Thinking Dress

Age	1-2 years	2-3 years	3-4 years
Size			
Back	27cm (10¾in) 45cm (17¾in)	30cm (11¾in) 48cm (19in)	32cm (12½in) 51cm (20¼in)
Front	40cm (15¾in)	42cm (16½in)	45cm (17¾in)

Yarn

Rowan All Seasons Cotton x 50g balls

Kiss	4	4	4

Needles

1 pair 4 mm (US 6) needles for edging
1 pair 5 mm (US 8) needles for main body

Tension

17 sts and 24 rows to 10cm measured over stocking stitch using 5 mm (US 8) needles

Note The chart is for the front only. Use it as a guide for the back as shaping and rows are the same.

Front

Using 4 mm (US 6) needles cast on 68,72,76 sts and work from chart and written instructions as folls:
Chart row 1: Knit.
Chart row 2: Knit.
Cont in garter st until chart row 6 completed.
Change to 5mm (US 8) needles work in st st and cable patt from chart as folls:
Chart row 7: Knit.
Chart row 8: P27,29,31, K2, P10, K2, P27,29,31.
Chart row 9 (inc): K30,32,34 (M1,K2) 4 times, M1, K30,32,34. (73,77,81 sts)
Chart row 10: P27,29,31, K2, P15, K2, P27,29,31.

Chart row 11: K32,34,36, C6F twice, K29,31,33.
Chart row 12: Work as given for row 10.
Chart row 13(dec): K2tog, knit to last 2 sts, K2tog. (71,75,79 sts)
Chart row 14: P26,28,30, K2, P15, K2, P26,28,30.
Chart row 15: K28,30,32, C6B twice, K31,33,35.
Chart row 16: Work as given for row 14.
Cont to work central cable patt and dec as indicated on chart to 51,55,59 sts.
Work without further shaping until chart row 84,90,94 completed.

Shape armhole

Cast off 4 sts at beginning next 2 rows. (43,47,51 sts)
Dec 1 st at each end of next 3 rows and 2 foll alt rows. (33,37,41 sts)

Ages 2-3 years and 3-4 years only

Work 3 rows in st st.
Dec 1 st at armhole edge on next row. (35,39 sts)

All ages

Work without further shaping to chart row 102,110,116 completed.

Shape front neck

Chart row 103,111,117: Knit 8,8,9 sts, turn and leave rem sts on a holder.
Dec 1 st at neck edge on next 3 rows. (5,5,6 sts)
Work without further shaping until chart row 110,118,124 completed.
Cast off rem sts.
Slip centre 17,19,21 sts onto a holder, rejoin yarn to rem sts, knit to end.
Dec 1 st at neck edge on next 3 rows. (5,5,6 sts)
Work without further shaping until chart row 110,118,124 completed. Cast off rem sts.

Back

Using 4 mm (US 6) needles cast on 68,72,76 sts and work **only** from written instructions as folls, using front chart as a guide for shaping and rows:
Row 1: Knit.
Row 2: Knit.
Cont in garter st until 6 rows in all completed.
Change to 5mm (US 8) needles work in st st as folls:
Row 7: Knit.
Row 8: Purl.
Work until 12 rows in all completed.
Row 13 (dec): K2tog, knit to last 2 sts, K2tog. (66,70,74 sts)
Work 5 rows in st st beg with a purl row.
Dec as above at each end of next row and every foll 6th row to 46,50,54 sts.
Work without further shaping until 84,90,94 rows in all completed.

Shape armhole and divide for back neck

Row 85,91,95: Cast off 4 sts at the beg next row, knit until there are 19,21,23 sts on RH needle, turn and leave rem sts on a holder.
Work each side of neck separately.
Row 86,92,96: Purl.
Dec 1 st at armhole edge on next 3 rows and 2 foll alt rows. (14,16,18 sts)

Ages 2-3 years and 3-4 years only

Work 3 rows in st st.
Dec 1 st at armhole edge on next row. (15,17 sts)

All ages

Work without shaping for a further 12,10,12 rows, and 105,113,119 rows in all completed.

Shape back neck

Row 106,114,120: Cast off 6,7,8 sts, purl to end. (8,8,9 sts)
Dec 1 st at neck edge on next 3 rows. (5,5,6 sts)
Work 1 row. Cast off rem sts.
Rejoin yarn to rem sts, knit to end. (23,25,27 sts)
Row 86,92,96: Cast off 4 sts at the beg next row, purl to end.
Dec 1 st at armhole edge on next 3 rows and 2 foll alt rows. (14,16,18 sts)

Ages 2-3 years and 3-4 years only

Work 3 rows in st st.
Dec 1 st at armhole edge on next row. (15,17 sts)

All ages

Work without shaping for a further 13,11,13 rows, and 106,114,120 rows in all completed.

Shape back neck

Chart row 107,115,121: Cast off 6,7,8 sts, knit to end. (8,8,9 sts)
Dec 1 sts at neck edge on next 3 rows.
Cast off rem 5,5,6 sts.

Press all pieces as shown in making up instructions, page 48.

Back neck opening

With RS facing and using 4 mm (US 6) needles pick up and K16,18,20 sts down right back neck opening and 16,18,20 sts up left back neck opening. (32,36,40 sts)
Cast off knitwise 14,16,18, (K2tog, cast off 1 st) twice cast off all rem sts.
Join both shoulder seams using backstitch.

Neck edging

With RS facing and using 4 mm (US 6) needles and starting at centre back pick up and knit 11,12,13 sts to shoulder, 8 sts down left front neck, work across

19,21 sts on front neck holder as folls:
2,3, (K1, K2tog) 5 times, K1,2,3, pick up
d knit 8 sts to shoulder, and 11,12,13 sts
centre back. (50,54,58 sts)
t 2 rows.
st off knitwise on a WS row.

rmhole edgings (both alike)
th RS facing and using 4 mm (US 6)
edles pick up and knit 25,27,29 sts from
e seam to shoulder and 25,27,29 sts
wn to side seam. (50,54,58 sts)
t 2 rows.
st off knitwise on a WS row.

aking up
ke a button loop at top opening on right
ck, sew button on left side to match.
n side seams.

☐ K on RS,
P on WS

⦿ P on RS,
K on WS

☑ M1

C6B

C6F

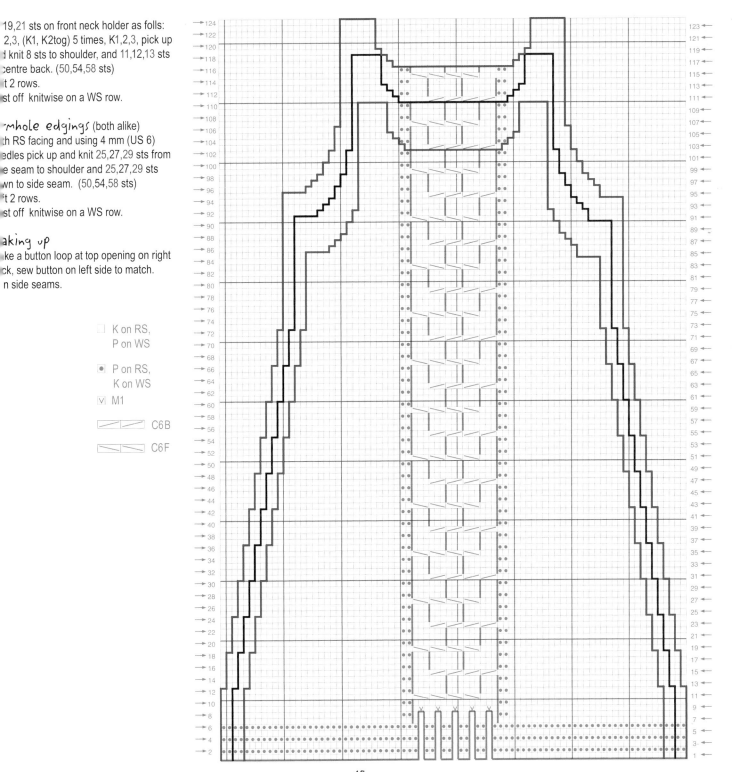

45

Out to Play Coat

Age	1-2 years	2-3 years	3-4 years
Size Back Front	36cm (14½in) 45cm (17¾in)	39cm (15¼in) 48cm (19in)	43cm (17in) 51cm (20¼in)
Size Sleeve	20cm (8in)	23.5cm (9¼in)	26.5cm (10½in)

Yarn

Rowan All Seasons Cotton x 50g balls

| Valour | 6 | 6 | 7 |

Needles

1 pair 4mm (US 6) needles for edging
1 pair 5mm (US 8) needles for main body

Buttons 5

Tension

17 sts and 24 rows to 10cm measured over stocking stitch using 5mm (US 8) needles

Note The charts are for coat fronts only. Work from written instructions for back and sleeves, using chart as a guide for back as shaping and rows are the same.

Left Front

Using 4mm (US 6) needles cast on 30,33,36 sts and work from chart and written instructions as folls:
Chart row 1: P1,0,1, (K1, P1) to last st, K1.
Chart row 2: (K1, P1) to last 0,1,0 st, K0,1,0.
These 2 rows set the sts for moss st.
Cont until chart row 10 completed.

Change to 5mm (US 8) needles and work in cable panel patt as indicted on chart for left front as folls:
Chart row 11: Knit
Chart row 12: P2. (K1, P4) twice, K1, purl to end.
Chart row 13 (inc): K19,22,25, M1, K2, M1, K3, M1, K2, M1, K4. (34,37,40 sts)
Chart row 14: P2. (K1, P6) twice, K1, purl to end.
Chart row 15: K18,21,24, C6B, K1, C6F, K3.
Chart row 16: P2, K1, P4, (K1, P1) 3 times, P3, K1, purl to end.
Cont to work in cable patt as set until chart row 78,84,88 completed.

Shape armhole

Cast off 5 sts at the beg next row. (29,32,35 sts)
Work until chart row 107,115,121 completed.

Shape front neck

Chart row 108,116,122: Cast off 9,10,11 sts, patt to end. (20,22,24 sts)
Work 1 row.
Chart row 110,118,124: Cast off 4 sts, patt to end.
Dec 1 st at neck edge on next 2 rows. (14,16,18 sts)

Shape shoulder

Cast off 5,5,6 sts at the beg next row and foll alt row. Work 1 row. Cast off rem 4,6,6 sts.

Right Front

Using 4mm (US 6) needles cast on 30,33,36 sts and work from chart and written instructions as folls:
Chart row 1: (K1, P1) to last 0,1,0 st, K0,1,0.
Chart row 2: P1,0,1, (K1, P1) to last st, K1.
These 2 rows set the sts for moss st.
Cont until chart row 10 completed.
Change to 5mm (US 8) needles and work cable panel patt as indicated on chart for right front as folls:
Chart row 11: Knit
Chart row 12: P17,20,23 (K1, P4) twice, K1, P2.
Chart row 13 (inc): K4, M1, K2, M1, K3, M1, K2, M1, knit to end. (34,37,40 sts)
Chart row 14: P17,20,23 (K1, P6) twice, K1, P2.
Chart row 15: K3, C6B, K1, C6F, knit to end.
Chart row 16: P17,20,23, K1, P4, (K1, P1) 3 times, P3, K1, P2.
Complete to match left front, foll chart for right front and reversing shaping.

Back

Using 4mm (US 6) needles cast on 61,67,73 sts and work from written instructions as folls:
Row 1: P1,0,1, (K1, P1) to last 0,1,0 sts, K0,1,0.
Row 2: K0,1,0, (P1, K1) to last 0,1,0 sts, P1,0,1.
Cont in moss st until 10 rows in all completed.
Change to 5mm (US 8) needles work in st st until 78,84,88 rows in all completed.

Shape armhole

Cast off 5 sts at the beg next 2 rows. (51,57,63 sts)
Work until 112,120,126 rows in all completed.

Shape shoulders and back neck

Cast off 5,5,6 sts at the beg next 2 rows. (41,47,51 sts)
Row 115,123,129: Cast off 5,5,6 sts, knit until 7,9,9 sts on RH needle, turn and leave rem sts on a holder.
Row 116,124,130: Cast off 3 sts, purl to end.
Cast off rem 4,6,6 sts.
Rejoin yarn and cast off centre 17,19,21 sts, knit to end
Row 116,124,130: Cast off 5,5,6 sts, purl to end. (7,9,9 sts)
Row 117,125,131: Cast off 3 sts, knit to end.
Cast off rem 4,6,6 sts.

Sleeves (both alike)

Using 4 mm (US 6) needles cast on 31,33,35 sts and work from written instructions as folls:
Row 1: (K1, P1) to last st, K1.
Row 2: (K1, P1) to last st, K1.
Cont in moss st until 10 rows in all completed.
Change to 5mm (US 8) needles work in st st as folls:
Row 11: Inc into first st, knit to last st, inc into last st. (33,35,37 sts)
Row 12: Purl.
Work 2 rows in st st.
Inc at each end of next row and every foll 4th row to 47,51,55 sts.
Work without further shaping until sleeve measures 20.5,23.5,26.5 cm from cast on edge. Cast off.

Press all pieces as shown on page 48.

Buttonhole band

With RS of right front facing and using 4 mm (US 6) needles pick up and knit 71,77,81 sts from cast on edge to start of neck shaping.
Row 1 (WS row): (K1, P1) to last st, K1.
Row 2: (K1, P1) to last st, K1.
Buttonhole row (WS row): Patt 7,8,9 (yo, patt 2tog, patt 12,13,14) 3 times, yo, patt 2tog, patt to end.
Work 2 more rows in moss st.
Cast off in moss st.

Buttonband

With RS of right front facing and using 4 mm (US 6) needles pick up and knit 71,77,81 sts from start of neck shaping to cast on edge.
Row 1 (WS row): (K1, P1) to last st, K1.
Work 4 more rows in moss st.
Cast off in moss st.

in both shoulder seams using backstitch.
th RS facing and using 4 mm (US 6) needles
k up and knit 4 sts across buttonhole band
,19,20 sts up right front neck shaping,
,25,27 sts across back neck, and 18,19,20 sts
wn left front neck, and 4 sts from buttonband.
,71,75 sts)

w 1 (WS): (K1, P1) to last st, K1.

ork 1 row in moss st.

ttonhole row (WS row): Patt to last 3 sts, yo,
t 2tog, patt 1.

rk 2 more rows in moss st.

st off in moss st.

mplete Jacket as shown on page 48.

w on buttons to correspond with buttonholes.

☐ K on RS,
P on WS

• P on RS,
K on WS

Ⓥ M1

⬛ C6B

⬛ C6F

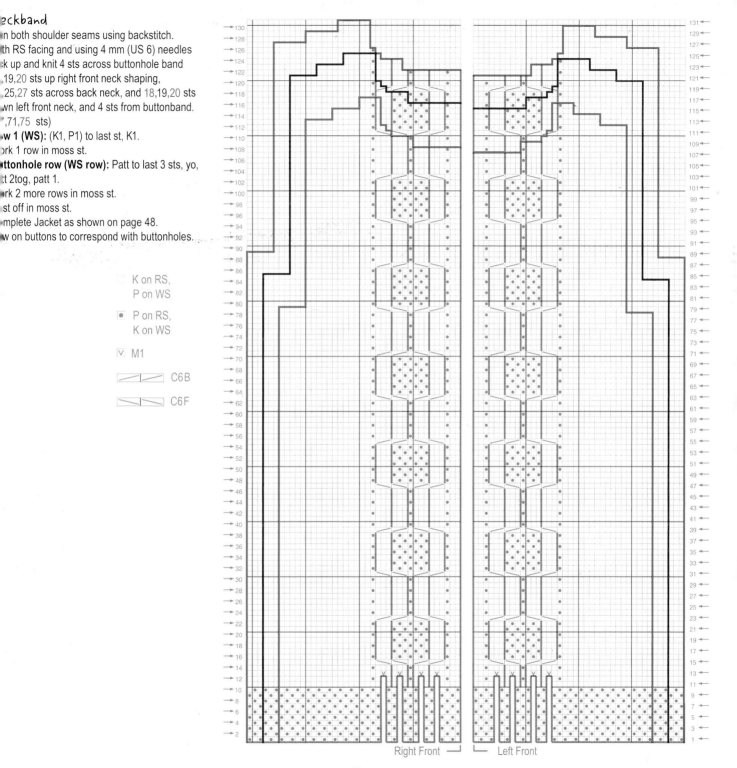

Right Front ⌐   ⌐ Left Front

47

Knitting Techniques
A simple guide to making up and finishing

Putting your garment together
After spending many hours knitting it is essential that you complete your garment correctly. Following the written instructions and illustrations we show you how easy it is to achieve a beautifully finished garment; which will withstand the most boisterous child.

Pressing
With the wrong side of the fabric facing, pin out each knitted garment piece onto an ironing board using the measurements given in the size diagram. As each yarn is different, refer to the ball band and press pieces according to instructions given. Pressing the knitted fabric will help the pieces maintain their shape and give a smooth finish.

Sewing in ends
Once you have pressed your finished pieces, sew in all loose ends. Thread a darning needle with yarn, weave needle along approx 5 sts on wrong side of fabric; pull thread through. Weave needle in opposite direction approx 5 sts; pull thread through, cut end of yarn.

Making Up
If you are making a sweater join the right shoulder seam as instructed in the pattern, now work the neck edging. Join left shoulder seam and neck edging. If you are making a cardigan, join both shoulder seams as in the pattern and work edgings as instructed. Sew on buttons to correspond with buttonholes. Insert square set in sleeves as follows: Sew cast off edge of sleeve top into armhole. Making a neat right angle, sew in the straight sides at top of sleeve to cast off stitches at armhole. Join side and sleeve seams using either mattress stitch or back stitch. It is important to press each of the seams as you make the garment up.

Casting Off shoulder Seams together
This method secures the front and back shoulder stitches together, it also creates a small ridged seam. It is important that the cast off edge should by elastic like the rest of the fabric; if you find that your cast off is too tight, try using a larger needle. You can cast off with the seam on the right side (as illustrated) or wrong side of garment.

1. Place wrong sides of fabric together. Hold both needles with the stitches on in LH, insert RH needle into first stitch on both LH needles.

2. Draw the RH needle through both stitches.

3. Making one stitch on RH needle.

4. Knit the next stitch from both LH needles, two stitches on RH needle.

5. Using the point of one needle in LH, insert into first stitch on RH needle. Take the first stitch over the second stitch.

6. Repeat from 4. until one stitch left on right hand needle. Cut yarn and draw cut end through stitch to secure.

Picking Up Stitches

Once you have finished all the garment pieces, pressed them and sewn in all ends, you need to complete the garment by adding a neckband, front bands, or armhole edgings. This is done by picking up stitches along the edge of the knitted piece. The number of stitches to pick up is given in the pattern; these are made using a new yarn. When you pick up horizontally along a row of knitting it is important that you pick up through a whole stitch. When picking up stitches along a row edge, pick up one stitch in from the edge, this gives a neat professional finish.

1. Holding work in LH, with RS of fabric facing, insert RH needle into a whole stitch below the cast off edge, wrap new yarn around needle.

2. Draw the RH needle through fabric; making a loop with new yarn on right hand needle.

3. Repeat this action into the next stitch following the pattern instructions until all stitches have been picked up.

4. Work edging as instructed.

Mattress Stitch

This method of sewing up is worked on the right side of the fabric and is ideal for matching stripes. Mattress stitch should be worked one stitch in from edge to give the best finish. With RS of work facing, lay the two pieces to be joined edge to edge. Insert needle from WS between edge st and second st. Take yarn to opposite piece, insert needle from front, pass the needle under two rows, bring it back through to the front.

1. Work mattress stitch foundation as above.

2. Return yarn to opposite side working under two rows at a time, repeat.

3. At regular intervals gently pull stitches together.

4. The finished seam is very neat and almost impossible to see.

Back stitch

This method of sewing up is ideal for shoulder and armhole seams as it does not allow the fabric to stretch out of shape. Pin the pieces with right sides together. Insert needle into fabric at end, one stitch or row from edge, take the needle round the two edges securing them. Insert needle into fabric just behind where last stitch came out and make a short stitch . Re-insert needle where previous stitch started, bring up needle to make a longer stitch. Re-insert needle where last stitch ended, repeat to end taking care to match any pattern.

Sewing in a Zip

With right side facing, neatly match row ends and slip stitch fronts of garment together.   Pin zip into place, with right side of zip to wrong side of garment, matching centre front of garment to centre of zip. Neatly backstitch into place using a matching coloured thread. Undo slip stitches, zip inserted.

Rowan Overseas Distributors

AUSTRALIA : Australian Country Spinners, 314 Albert Street, Brunswick, Victoria 3056. Tel : (03) 9380 3888

BELGIUM : Pavan, Koningin Astridlaan 78, B9000 Gent. Tel : (32) 9 221 8594
E mail: pavan@pandora.be

CANADA: Diamond Yarn, 9697 St Laurent, Montreal, Quebec, H3L 2N1. Tel :(514) 388 6188
Diamond Yarn (Toronto), 155 Martin Ross, Unit 3, Toronto, Ontario,M3J 2L9. Tel :(416) 736 6111
E mail: diamond@diamondyarn.com

DENMARK : Please contact Rowan for stockist details.

FRANCE : Elle Tricot, 8 Rue du Coq, 67000 Strasbourg. Tel : (33) 3 88 23 03 13.
E mail: elletricot@wanadoo.fr

GERMANY : Wolle & Design, Wolfshovener Strasse 76, 52428 Julich-Stetternich. Tel : (49) 2461 54735.
E mail : Wolle_und_Design@t-online.de

HOLLAND : de Afstap, Oude Leliestraat 12, 1015 AW Amsterdam. Tel : (31) 20 6231445.

HONG KONG : East Unity Co Ltd, Unit B2, 7/F, Block B, Kailey Industrial Centre, 12 Fung Yip Street, Chai Wan. Tel : (852) 2869 7110.

ICELAND : Storkurinn, Kjorgardi, Laugavegi 59, Reykjavik. Tel : (354) 551 82 58.

JAPAN : Puppy Co Ltd, TOC Building, 7-22-17 Nishigotanda, Shinagawa-ku, Tokyo. Tel : (81) 3 3494 2395.
E mail: webmaster@puppyarn.co.jp

KOREA : My Knit Studio, (3F) 121 Kwan Hoon Dong, Chongro-ku, Seoul. Tel : (82) 2 722 0006

NEW ZEALAND : Please contact Rowan for stockist details.

NORWAY : Pa Pinne, Tennisvn 3D, 0777 Oslo. Tel : (47) 909 62 818.
E mail : design@paapinne.no

SWEDEN : Wincent, Norrtulsgaten 65, 11345 Stockholm. Tel : (46) 8 673 70 60 Fax: (46) 8 33 70 68.
E mail: wincent@chello.se

TAIWAN : Il Lisa International Trading Co Ltd, No 181, Sec 4, Chung Ching N. Road, Taipei, Taiwan R.O.C. Tel : (886) 2 8221 2925.
Chien He Wool Knitting Co, 10 -1 313 Lane, Sec 3, Cmung-Ching North Road, Taipei, Taiwan. Tel : (886) 2 2596 0269

U.S.A.: Rowan USA, 4 Townsend West, Suite 8, Nashua, New Hampshire 03063. Tel : (1 603) 886 5041 / 5043.
E mail : wfibers@aol.com

UNITED KINGDOM : Green Lane Mill, Holmfirth,West Yorkshire, HD9 2DX. Tel : (44) (0) 1484 681881.
Email : mail@knitrowan.com